BEST KARATE 6

Bassai, Kankū

M. Nakayama

KODANSHA INTERNATIONAL LTD.

Tokyo, New York & San Francisco

Front cover photo by Keizō Kaneko; demonstration photos by Yoshinao Murai.

Distributed in the United States by Kodansha International/USA Ltd., through Harper & Row, Publishers, Inc., 10 East 53rd Street, New York, New York 10022.

Published by Kodansha International Ltd., 12−21 Otowa 2-chome, Bunkyo-ku, Tokyo 112 and Kodansha International/USA Ltd., 10 East 53rd Street, New York, New York 10022 and 44 Montgomery Street, San Francisco, California 94104. Copyright © 1979 by Kodansha International Ltd. All rights reserved. Printed in Japan.
LCC 77−74827
ISBN 0−87011−383−6
ISBN 4−7700−0738−8 (in Japan)

First edition, 1979
Second printing, 1982

CONTENTS

Introduction   9
What Karate-dō Is   11
Kata   12
  Meaning, Important Points, Bassai and Kankū
Bassai   15
  Important Points, *64*
Kankū   67
  Important Points, *138*
Glossary   *142*

Dedicated
to my teacher
GICHIN FUNAKOSHI

The past decade has seen a great increase in the popularity of karate-dō throughout the world. Among those who have been attracted to it are college students and teachers, artists, businessmen and civil servants. It has come to be practiced by policemen and members of Japan's Self-defense Forces. In a number of universities, it has become a compulsory subject, and that number is increasing yearly.

Along with the increase in popularity, there have been certain unfortunate and regrettable interpretations and performances. For one thing, karate has been confused with the so-called Chinese-style boxing, and its relationship with the original Okinawan *Te* has not been sufficiently understood. There are also people who have regarded it as a mere show, in which two men attack each other savagely, or the contestants battle each other as though it were a form of boxing in which the feet are used, or a man shows off by breaking bricks or other hard objects with his head, hand or foot.

If karate is practiced solely as a fighting technique, this is cause for regret. The fundamental techniques have been developed and perfected through long years of study and practice, but to make any effective use of these techniques, the spiritual aspect of this art of self-defense must be recognized and must play the predominant role. It is gratifying to me to see that there are those who understand this, who know that karate-dō is a purely Oriental martial art, and who train with the proper attitude.

To be capable of inflicting devastating damage on an opponent with one blow of the fist or a single kick has indeed been the objective of this ancient Okinawan martial art. But even the practitioners of old placed stronger emphasis on the spiritual side of the art than on the techniques. Training means training of body and spirit, and, above all else, one should treat his opponent courteously and with the proper etiquette. It is not enough to fight with all one's power; the real objective in karate-dō is to do so for the sake of justice.

Gichin Funakoshi, a great master of karate-dō, pointed out repeatedly that the first purpose in pursuing this art is the nurturing of a sublime spirit, a spirit of humility. Simultaneously, power sufficient to destroy a ferocious wild animal with a single blow should be developed. Becoming a true follower of karate-dō is possible only when one attains perfection in these two aspects, the one spiritual, the other physical.

Karate as an art of self-defense and karate as a means of improving and maintaining health has long existed. During the past twenty years, a new activity has been explored and is coming to the fore. This is *sports karate.*

In sports karate, contests are held for the purpose of determining the ability of the participants. This needs emphasizing, for here again there is cause for regret. There is a tendency to place too much emphasis on winning contests, and those who do so neglect the practice of fundamental techniques, opting instead to attempt jiyū kumite at the earliest opportunity.

Emphasis on winning contests cannot help but alter the fundamental techniques a person uses and the practice he engages in. Not only that, it will result in a person's being incapable of executing a strong and effective technique, which, after all, is the unique characteristic of karate-dō. The man who begins jiyū kumite prematurely—without having practiced fundamentals sufficiently—will soon be overtaken by the man who has trained in the basic techniques long and diligently. It is, quite simply, a matter of haste makes waste. There is no alternative to learning and practicing basic techniques and movements step by step, stage by stage.

If karate competitions are to be held, they must be conducted under suitable conditions and in the proper spirit. The desire to win a contest is counterproductive, since it leads to a lack of seriousness in learning the fundamentals. Moreover, aiming for a savage display of strength and power in a contest is totally undesirable. When this happens, courtesy toward the opponent is forgotten, and this is of prime importance in any expression of karate. I believe this matter deserves a great deal of reflection and self-examination by both instructors and students.

To explain the many and complex movements of the body, it has been my desire to present a fully illustrated book with an up-to-date text, based on the experience in this art that I have acquired over a period of forty-six years. This hope is being realized by the publication of the *Best Karate* series, in which earlier writings of mine have been totally revised with the help and encouragement of my readers. This new series explains in detail what karate-dō is in language made as simple as possible, and I sincerely hope that it will be of help to followers of karate-dō. I hope also that karateka in many countries will be able to understand each other better through this series of books.

WHAT KARATE-DŌ IS

Deciding who is the winner and who is the loser is not the ultimate objective. Karate-dō is a martial art for the development of character through training, so that the karateka can surmount any obstacle, tangible or intangible.

Karate-dō is an empty-handed art of self-defense in which the arms and legs are systematically trained and an enemy attacking by surprise can be controlled by a demonstration of strength like that of using actual weapons.

Karate-dō is exercise through which the karateka masters all body movements, such as bending, jumping and balancing, by learning to move limbs and body backward and forward, left and right, up and down, freely and uniformly.

The techniques of karate-dō are well controlled according to the karateka's will power and are directed at the target accurately and spontaneously.

The essence of karate techniques is *kime*. The meaning of *kime* is an explosive attack to the target using the appropriate technique and maximum power in the shortest time possible. (Long ago, there was the expression *ikken hissatsu*, meaning "to kill with one blow," but to assume from this that killing is the objective is dangerous and incorrect. It should be remembered that the karateka of old were able to practice *kime* daily and in dead seriousness by using the makiwara.)

Kime may be accomplished by striking, punching or kicking, but also by blocking. A technique lacking *kime* can never be regarded as true karate, no matter how great the resemblance to karate. A contest is no exception; however, it is against the rules to make contact because of the danger involved.

Sun-dome means to arrest a technique just before contact with the target (one *sun*, about three centimeters). But not carrying a technique through to *kime* is not true karate, so the question is how to reconcile the contradiction between *kime* and *sun-dome*. The answer is this: establish the target slightly in front of the opponent's vital point. It can then be hit in a controlled way with maximum power, without making contact.

Training transforms various parts of the body into weapons to be used freely and effectively. The quality necessary to accomplish this is self-control. To become a victor, one must first overcome his own self.

KATA

The *kata* of karate-dō are logical arrangements of blocking, punching, striking and kicking techniques in certain set sequences. About fifty kata, or "formal exercises," are practiced at the present time, some having been passed down from generation to generation, others having been developed fairly recently.

Kata can be divided into two broad categories. In one group are those appropriate for physical development, the strengthening of bone and muscle. Though seemingly simple, they require composure for their performance and exhibit strength and dignity when correctly performed. In the other group are kata suitable for the development of fast reflexes and the ability to move quickly. The lightninglike movements in these kata are suggestive of the rapid flight of the swallow. All kata require and foster rhythm and coordination.

Training in kata is spiritual as well as physical. In his performance of the kata, the karateka should exhibit boldness and confidence, but also humility, gentleness and a sense of decorum, thus integrating mind and body in a singular discipline. As Gichin Funakoshi often reminded his students, "The spirit of karate-dō is lost without courtesy."

One expression of this courtesy is the bow made at the beginning and at the end of each kata. The stance is the *musubi-dachi* (informal attention stance), with the arms relaxed, the hands lightly touching the thighs and the eyes focused straight ahead.

From the bow at the start of the kata, one moves into the *kamae* of the first movement of the kata. This is a relaxed position, so tenseness, particularly in the shoulders and knees, should be eliminated and breathing should be relaxed. The center of power and concentration is the *tanden*, the center of gravity. In this position, the karateka should be prepared for any eventuality and full of fighting spirit.

Being relaxed but alert also characterizes the bow at the end of the kata and is called *zanshin*. In karate-dō, as in other martial arts, bringing the kata to a perfect finish is of the greatest importance.

Each kata begins with a blocking technique and consists of a specific number of movements to be performed in a particular order. There is some variation in the complexity of the movements and the time required to complete them, but each movement has its own meaning and function and nothing is superfluous. Performance is along the *embusen* (performance line), the shape of which is decided for each kata.

While performing a kata, the karateka should imagine himself to be surrounded by opponents and be prepared to execute defensive and offensive techniques in any direction.

Mastery of kata is a prerequisite for advancement through *kyū* and *dan* as follows:

8th *kyū*	Heian 1
7th *kyū*	Heian 2
6th *kyū*	Heian 3
5th *kyū*	Heian 4
4th *kyū*	Heian 5
3rd *kyū*	Tekki 1
2nd *kyū*	Kata other than Heian or Tekki
1st *kyū*	Other than the above
1st *dan*	Other than the above
2nd *dan* and above	Free kata

Free kata may be chosen from Bassai, Kankū, Jitte, Hangetsu, Empi, Gankaku, Jion, Tekki, Nijūshihō, Gojūshihō, Unsu, Sōchin, Meikyō, Chintei, Wankan and others.

Important Points

Since the effects of practice are cumulative, practice every day, even if only for a few minutes. When performing a kata, keep calm and never rush through the movements. This means always being aware of the correct timing of each movement. If a particular kata proves difficult, give it more attention, and always keep in mind the relationship between kata practice and kumite (see Vols. 3 and 4).

Specific points in performance are:

1. *Correct order.* The number and sequence of movements is predetermined. All must be performed.

2. *Beginning and end.* The kata must begin and end at the same spot on the *embusen.* This requires practice.

3. *Meaning of each movement.* Each movement, defensive or offensive must be clearly understood and fully expressed. This is also true of the kata as a whole, each of which has its own characteristics.

4. *Awareness of the target.* The karateka must know what the target is and when to execute a technique.

5. *Rhythm and timing.* Rhythm must be appropriate to the particular kata and the body must be flexible, never overstrained. Remember the three factors of the correct use of power, swiftness or slowness in executing techniques, and the stretching and contraction of muscles.

6. *Proper breathing.* Breathing should change with changing situations, but basically inhale when blocking, exhale

when a finishing technique is executed, and inhale and exhale when executing successive techniques.

Related to breathing is the *kiai*, which occurs in the middle or at the end of the kata, at the moment of maximum tension. By exhaling very sharply and tensing the abdomen, extra power can be given to the muscles.

Bassai and Kankū

Bassai and Kankū are both representative Shōtōkan kata.

From Bassai can be learned composure and agility, strength and change, fast and slow techniques, the dynamics of strength, turning disadvantage into advantage and changing blocks.

From Kankū can be learned fast and slow techniques, the dyamics of strength, body flexibility, rotation, jumping and going to ground.

It is important to learn them after learning the fundamentals through the Heian and Tekki kata, as they are both selected for Japan Karate Association matches. However strenuous the practice of them may be, keep in mind that they can be mastered.

Rhythm

BASSAI

1 2 · 3 4 · 5 6 · 7 8 9 10 · 11 12 · 13 14 15 16 · 17 18 19 20

21 22 23 · 24 25 26 26 28 29 · 30 · 31 32 33 34 35 36 37 38 39

40 41 42 ▲

KANKU

1 · 2 3 · 4 5 6 · 7 8 · 9 10 · 11 12 13 14 15 ▲ 16 17 · 18 · 19 20

21 22 · 23 · 24 25 26 · 27 · 28 29 · 30 · 31 32 33 34 35 36

37 · 38 39 · 40 · 41 42 · 43 44 45 46 · 47 48 · 49 · 50 51 · 52 53 54 55 · 56

57 58 59 60 · 61 62 63 64 · 65 ▲

Symbol	Meaning	Symbol	Meaning
⌢ (dotted)	continuous, fast	—	powerfully
⌢	strong, continuous, fast	◄ (curved)	slow, powerfully
⌣	strong	▲ ▲	pause
◄	increasingly strong	𝄆	*kiai*

14

1
BASSAI

From bow to yōi

From *shizen-tai*, bring left foot half a step inward, then right foot. Wrap left hand lightly around right fist.

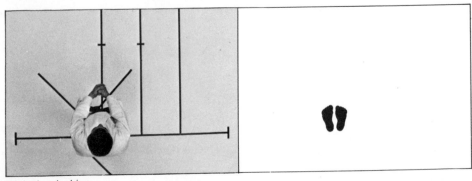

Heisoku-dachi

1

Migi chūdan uchi uke
Hidari shō migi tekubi yoko ni soeru

Right middle level block, inside outward/Left palm at right wrist Jump half a step to the front. Left foot behind right heel.

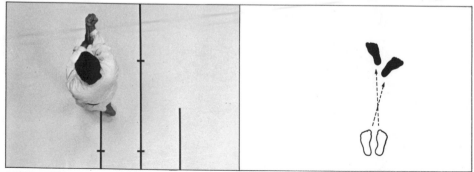

1. *Migi ashi mae kōsa-dachi*

2 *Hidari chūdan uchi uke*

Left middle level block, inside outward With right leg as pivot, block while turning hips to the left.

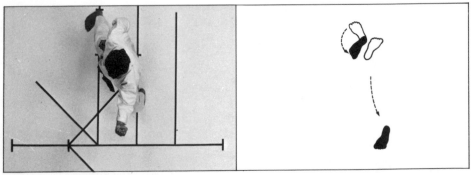

2. *Hidari zenkutsu-dachi*

3 Migi chūdan uchi uke

Right middle level block, inside outward

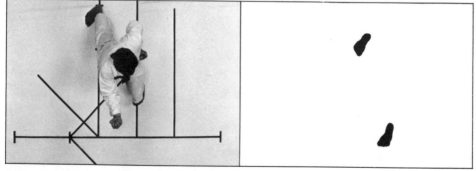

3.

4 Hidari chūdan soto uke

Left middle level block, outside inward With left leg as pivot, reverse direction by turning hips to the right.

4. Migi zenkutsu-dachi

5   *Migi chūdan uchi uke*

Right middle level block, inside outward

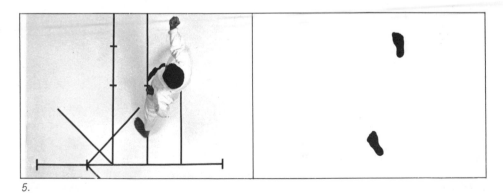

5.

Migi chūdan soto uke

Right middle level block, outside inward   Bring right foot in an arc near left foot. Block with thumb side of right wrist, in a wide downward motion, then forward from right shoulder.

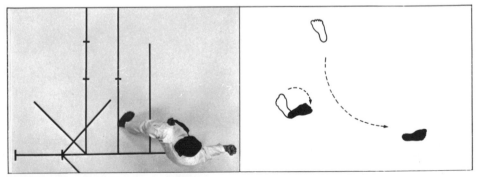

6. *Migi zenkutsu-dachi*

7 Hidari chūdan uchi uke
Gyaku hanmi

Left middle level block, inside outward/Reverse half-front-facing position Rotate hips to the right.

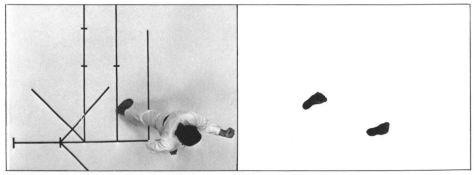

7. *Migi zenkutsu-dachi*

Ryō ken migi koshi kamae

Both fists at right side kamae Left fist (back frontward) on right fist (back downward). Face front, straighten knees.

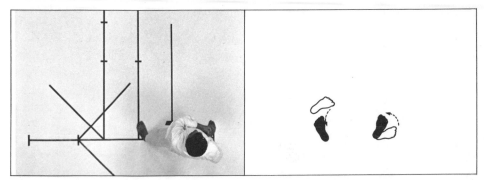

8 Hachinoji-dachi

9 Hidari tate shutō chūdan uchi uke

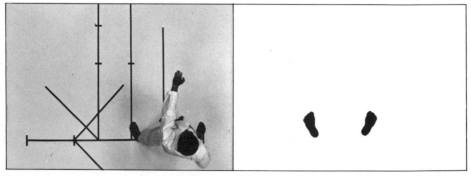

Left middle level vertical sword hand block, inside outward
Slowly describe arc to the front while straightening elbow.

9.

10 Migi ken chūdan choku-zuki

Middle level straight punch with right fist

10.

11 Migi chūdan uchi uke

Right middle level block, inside outward Keep feet in place, rotate hips to the left. Straighten right knee.

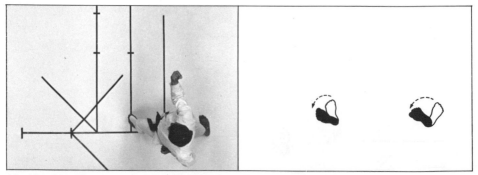

11. Hidari hiza kussu

12 Hidari ken chūdan choku-zuki

Middle level straight punch with left fist

12. Hachinoji-dachi

13 *Hidari chūdan uchi uke*

Left middle level block, inside outward Rotate hips to the right.

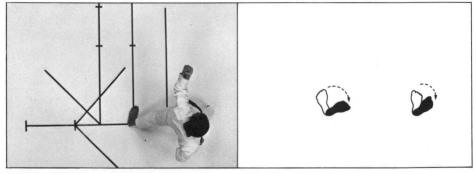

13. *Migi hiza kussu*

Migi shutō chūdan uke

Right sword hand middle level block With left leg as pivot, rotate hips to the left.

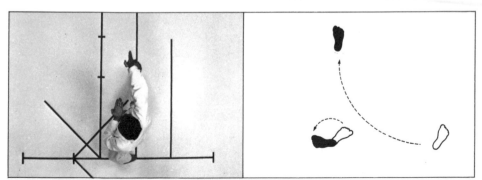

14. *Hidari kōkutsu-dachi*

Hidari shutō chūdan uke

Left sword hand middle level block   Slide left foot one step forward.

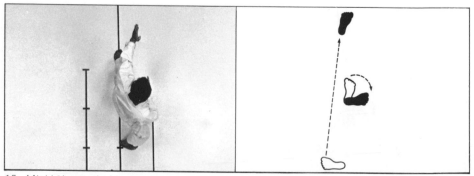

15. Migi kōkutsu-dachi

16 Migi shutō chūdan uke

Right sword hand middle level block Slide right foot one step
forward.

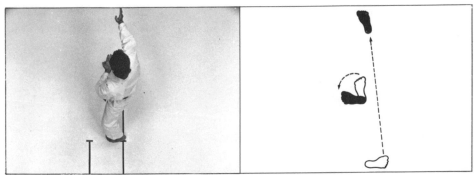

16. Hidari kōkutsu-dachi

17 Hidari shutō chūdan uke

Left sword hand middle level block
back.   Bring right foot one step

17. Migi kōkutsu-dachi

18 Ryō shō tsukami uke

Grasping block with both hands Both palms downward. Describe arc to the front with right hand from under left elbow.

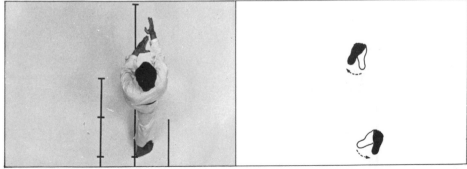

18. Hidari mae hiza yaya kussu

19 Ryǒ shō tsukamiyose
Migi sokutō gedan kekomi

Grasping-pulling with both palms/Lower level thrust kick with
right sword foot   Both palms downward.

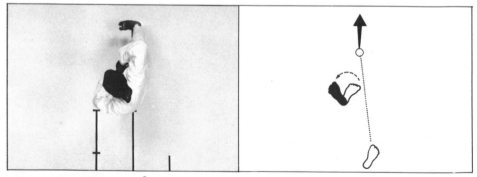

19. Hidari ashi-dachi

20 *Hidari shutō chūdan uke*

Left sword hand middle level block   Rotate hips to the left.
Lower kicking leg while turning to the rear.

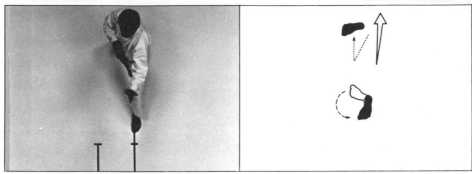

20. Migi kōkutsu-dachi

21 *Migi shutō chūdan uke*

Right sword hand middle level block
forward.

Move right foot one step

21. *Hidari kōkutsu-dachi*

Morote jōdan uke

Upper level block with both hands Back of both fists to the rear. Touch hands above face at same time foot is fully withdrawn.

22. *Heisoku-dachi*

23 | *Ryō kentsui chūdan hasami-uchi*

Middle level scissors strike with both hammer fists Slide right foot one step forward.

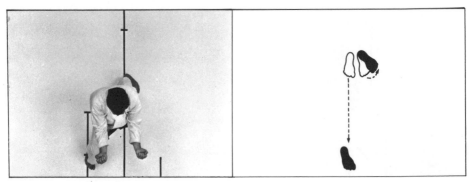

23. Migi zenkutsu-dachi

Middle level punch with right fist Slide feet forward (*yori-ashi*).

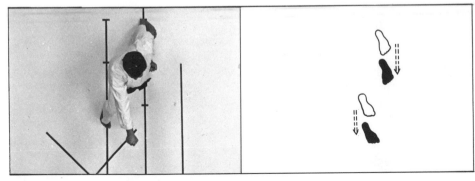

24.

25 a *Migi shutō gedan uchi-komi*
Hidari shō migi kata ue nagashi-uke

Lower level strike with right sword hand/Upper level sweeping block, left hand to right shoulder   Right leg is pivot.

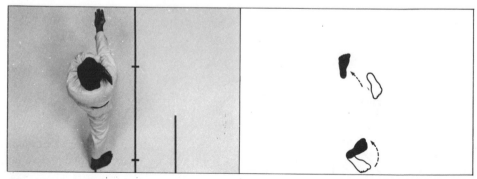

25a. *Hidari mae hiza kussu*

25 **b** *Migi ken migi sokumen jōdan uchi uke*
Hidari ken hidari sokumen gedan uke

Upper level block, inside outward, to right side with right fist/
Downward block to left side with left fist Only face to front.

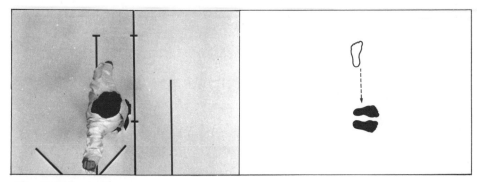

25b. Heisoku-dachi

Migi ken migi sokumen gedan uke

Downward block to right side with right fist   Left leg as pivot, turn hips to left.

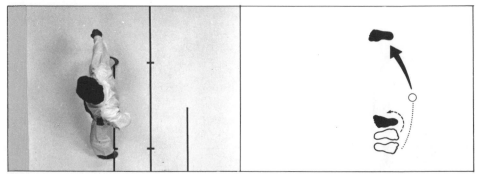

26. Kiba-dachi

Hidari shō hidari sokumen chūdan kake-uke

Middle level hooking block to left side with left palm Cross arms in front of chest.

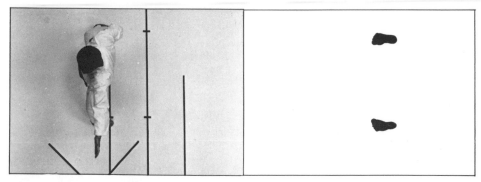

27.

28 a *Migi mikazuki-geri*

Right crescent kick Raise right knee high. Kicking in the shape of a crescent moon, strike left palm with right sole.

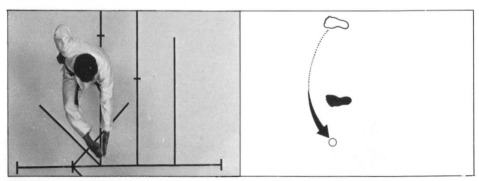

28a. *Hidari ashi-dachi*

Migi empi chūdan mae uchi

Middle level right elbow strike to the front Keeping left hand in place, strike left palm with right elbow.

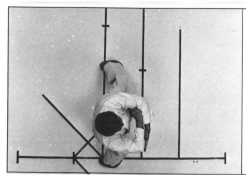

28b. Kiba-dachi

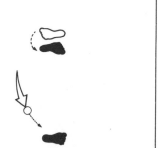

29 *Migi gedan barai*
Hidari ude mune mae kamae

30 *Hidari gedan barai*
Migi ude mune mae kamae

Right downward block/Left arm in front
of chest kamae

Left downward block/Right arm in
front of chest kamae

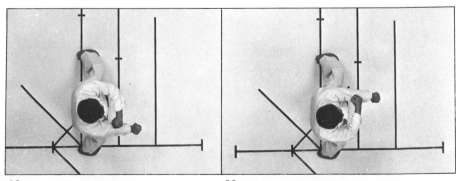

29.   30.

31 *Migi gedan barai*
Hidari ude mune mae kamae

Right downward block/Left arm in front of chest kamae   Backs of both fists to the front. Essentially like previous movement.

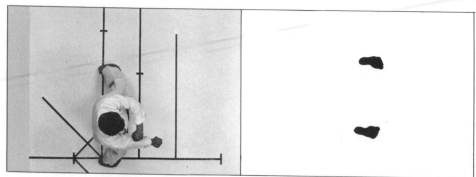

31.

32 *Ryō ken hidari koshi kamae*

Both fists left side kamae Right fist (back frontward) on left fist (back downward). Both feet in place, turn hips to the right.

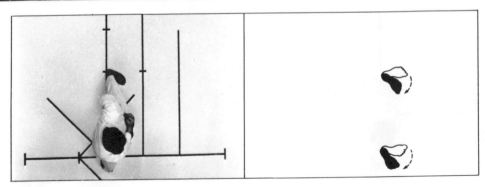

32. *Migi mae hiza kussu*

33 Yama-zuki (Hidari ken jōdan-zuki/Migi ken gedan ura-zuki)

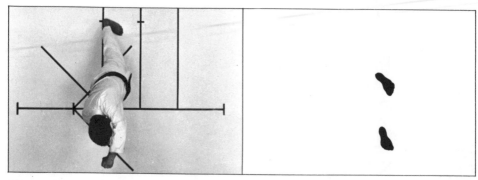

Wide U punch (Upper level punch with left fist/Lower level close punch with right fist)

33.

Both fists right side kamae Left fist on top. Bring right foot to left.

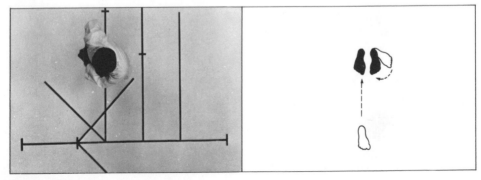

34. Heisoku-dachi

35 Yama-zuki (Migi ken jōdan-zuki/Hidari ken gedan ura-zuki)

Wide U punch (Upper level punch with right fist/Lower level close punch with left fist)

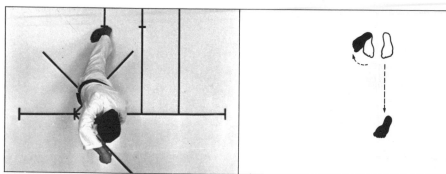

35. Hidari mae hiza kussu

36 *Ryō ken hidari koshi kamae*

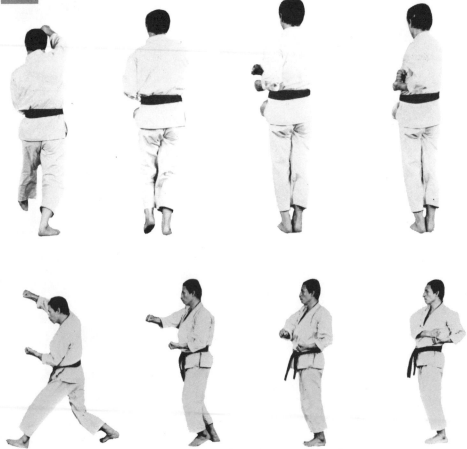

Both fists left side kamae Bring left foot back to right foot.

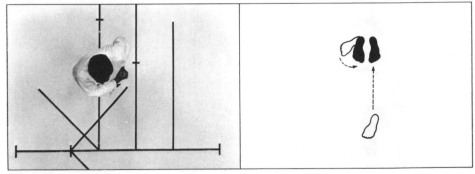

36. Heisoku-dachi

Yama-zuki (Hidari ken jōdan-zuki/Migi ken gedan ura-zuki)

Wide U punch (Upper level punch with left fist/Lower level close punch with right fist)

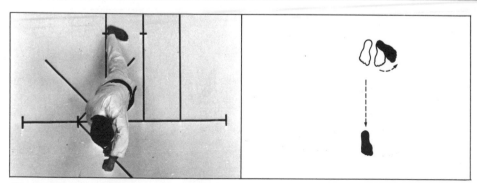

37. *Migi mae hiza kussu*

Right downward scooping block   With right leg as pivot,
rotate hips strongly to the left, left shoulder well to the rear,

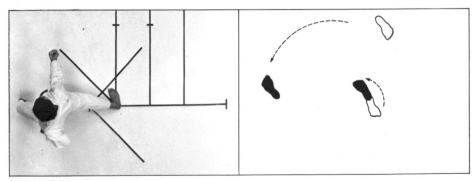

38. Hidari hiza kussu

right shoulder forward. Swing right fist widely from left shoulder
(back frontward), then straight front (back downward).

39 *Hidari gedan sukui-uke*

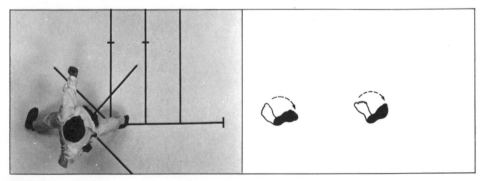

Left downward scooping block With feet in place, rotate hips to the right.

39. Migi hiza kussu

Right sword hand middle level block   Bring left foot directly under body, turn hips left. Slide right foot diagonally forward.

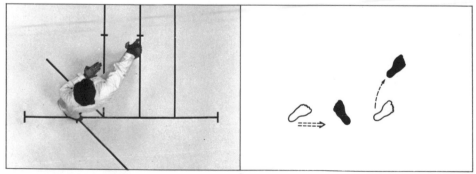

40. *Hidari kōkutsu-dachi*

Upper body as is   With left leg as pivot, slowly but strongly turn right hand, right leg to the right, head only diagonally left.

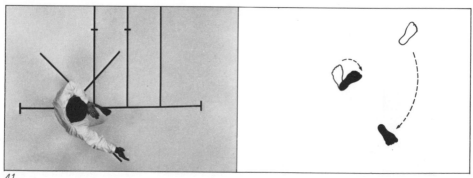

41.

42 *Hidari shutō chūdan uke*

Left sword hand middle level block Withdraw left leg half a step.

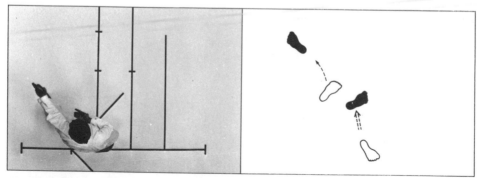

42. *Migi kōkutsu-dachi*

Yame

Withdraw left leg, return to position of readiness.

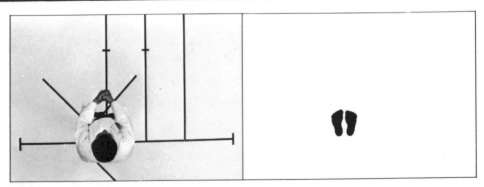

Heisoku-dachi

BASSAI: IMPORTANT POINTS

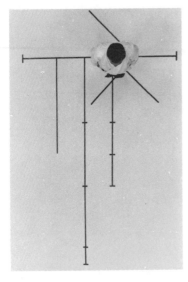

Bassai is so called because it presupposes the spirit and strength necessary to break into an enemy stronghold. It must be full of vitality, but if it does not have imposing dignity, its special characteristics will not come out. It and Kankū are bright jewels among Shōtōkan kata. After learning fundamentals from the basic kata, this is one to be mastered by all means.

Learn how to use opposites: composure and agility, strength and change, fast and slow techniques, light and heavy applications of strength. Otherwise it will not be effective.

The *embusen* is T shaped.

Forty-two movements. About one minute.

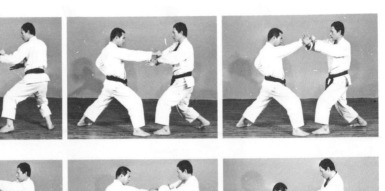

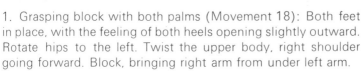

1. Grasping block with both palms (Movement 18): Both feet in place, with the feeling of both heels opening slightly outward. Rotate hips to the left. Twist the upper body, right shoulder going forward. Block, bringing right arm from under left arm.

2. Grasping-pulling with both palms: Strong stamping kick diagonally frontward with right sword foot. Simultaneously clench both fists (backs upward) in front of right side of chest, pull back strongly.

3. Middle level scissors strike with both hammer fists: Blocking the opponent's two-fist punch with both hands, immediately lower arms, step forward (*fumidashi*). Strike opponent's sides with hammer fists in a pincer movement. Open arms as little as possible, but strongly. If arms are opened widely, there is the possibility of the same kind of attack from the opponent.

4. Crescent kick: In the right crescent kick, raise the knee as high as possible, have the feeling of swinging the right foot. Avoid lifting the left hand or bringing it closer to the foot. Keep left hand in place.

5. Movements 29, 30, 31: Posture and elbows as they are. At the time of beating downward with the right fist, keep left fist in place (backs of both fists frontward) in front of the chest. Alternate fists.

6

7

6. *Yama-zuki* (Movements 33–37): This is a counterattack for such times as being grabbed by the hair. Without trying to free your head, twist the body with the feeling of falling to the side. Stare at the opponent and counterattack to the abdomen and just below the nose at the same time.

7. Downward scooping block, (Movements 38, 39): Immediately on blocking the opponent's foot with the thumb side of the wrist (back of fist frontward) you should have the feeling of abandoning the block (back of fist turning downward).

8. Changing direction (Movement 40): Because of changing direction to respond to an opponent diagonally to the front, block with the sword hand while drawing the left foot directly under the torso. This is the same principle as in Movement 7 of Heian 2.

2
KANKŪ

From bow to yōi

Slowly and quietly bring the hands together, placing the right fingertips on the left hand.

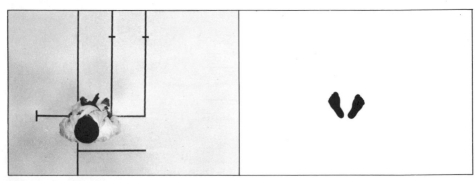

Shizen-tai.

1 *Ryō shō kasaneta mama hitai naname ue ni*

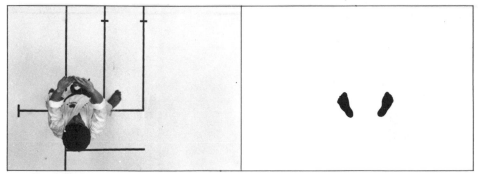

Hands together diagonally above the forehead Both palms outward. Look through the fingers at the sky.

1. Hachinoji-dachi

2 *Ittan ryō shō sayū ni hiraki*
Ryō shō kafukubu mae e

Open hands to the sides/Both hands in front of abdomen
Forcefully for an instant, then naturally and quietly, lower

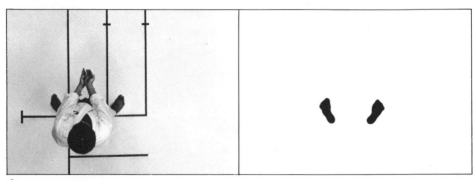

2.

hands. Straighten elbows lightly and quietly. Bring palms diagonally outward, right in front of left.

3

*Hidari haiwan hidari sokumen jōdan uke
Migi shō mune mae kamae*

Upper level block to left side with upper side of forearm/Right palm in front of chest *kamae* Left palm frontward.

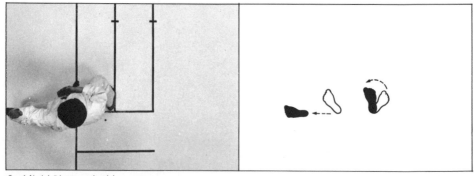

3. *Migi kōkutsu-dachi*

4 *Migi haiwan migi sokumen jōdan uke*
Hidari shō mune mae kamae

Upper level block to right side with upper side of right forearm/
Left palm in front of chest kamae   Movements 3, 4 very rapid.

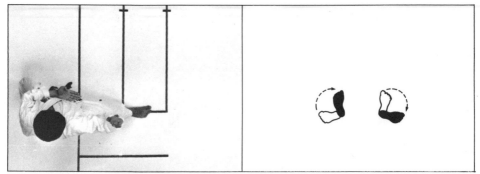

4. Hidari kōkutsu-dachi

5 *Hidari tate shutō chūdan uchi uke*
Migi ken migi koshi

Middle level block, inside outward, with left vertical sword hand/Right fist at right side Feet in place, straighten knees.

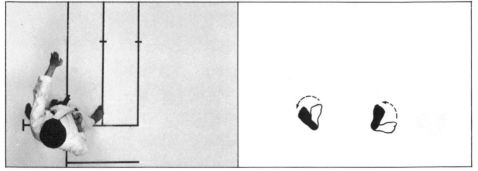

5. Hachinoji-dachi

6 *Migi ken chūdan choku-zuki*

Middle level straight punch with right fist

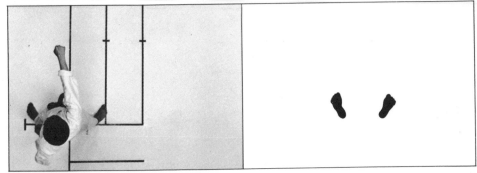

6.

7 Migi chūdan uchi uke

Right middle level block, inside outward Describe a circle with elbow as the center. No power in right elbow.

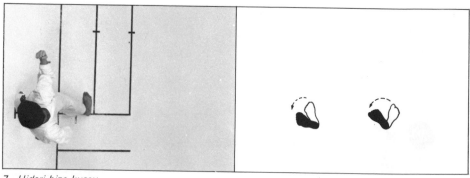

7. *Hidari hiza kussu*

Left middle level straight punch   Rotate hips to the right.

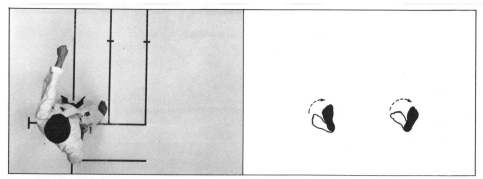

8. *Hachinoji-dachi*

Hidari chūdan uchi uke

Left middle level block, inside outward

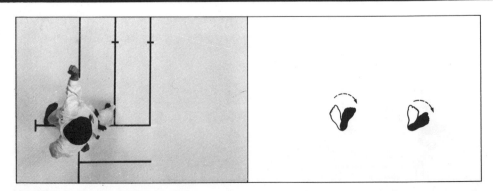

9. Migi hiza kussu

10 | *Ryō ken hidari koshi kamae*

Both fists left side kamae Right fist (back frontward) on left
fist (back downward).

10. *Hidari ashi-dachi*

11 *Migi uraken jōdan yoko mawashi-uchi*
Migi yoko keage

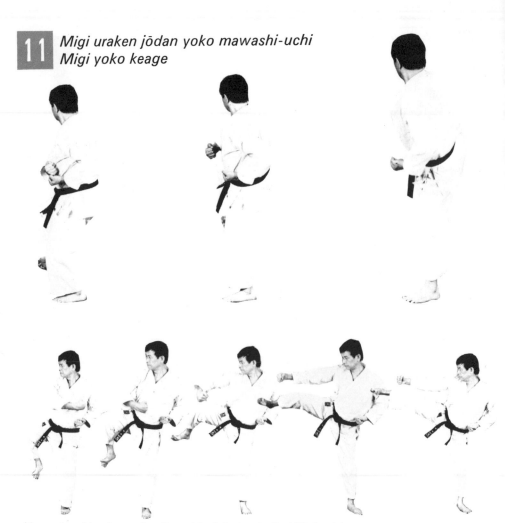

Upper level horizontal strike with right back-fist / Right side snap
kick

11.

Hidari shutō chūdan uke

Left sword hand middle level block Lower kicking foot, turn
to the rear.

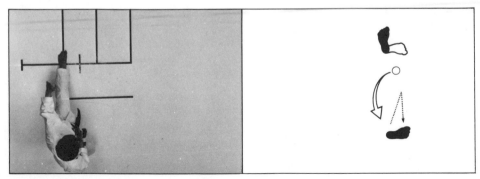

12. Migi kōkutsu-dachi

13 *Migi shutō chūdan uke*

Right sword hand middle level block Advance one step forward.

13. *Hidari kōkutsu-dachi*

Hidari shutō chūdan uke

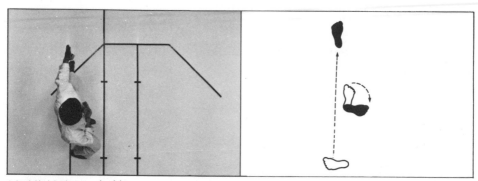

Left sword hand middle level block Advance one step forward.

14. *Migi kōkutsu-dachi*

15 Migi nukite chūdan-zuki
Hidari shō osae-uke

Right spear hand middle level punch/Pressing block with left palm Advance one step forward.

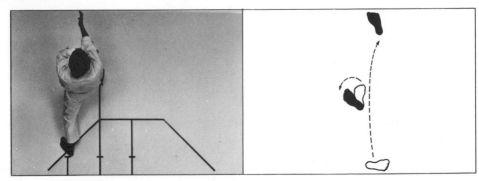

15. Migi zenkutsu-dachi

16

Migi shutō jōdan yoko mawashi-uchi
Hidari shō hitai mae jōdan uke/Gyaku hanmi

Upper level horizontal strike with right sword hand/Upper level
block, left palm in front of forehead/Reverse half-front-facing
position

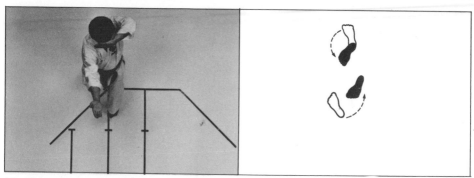

16. *Hidari mae hiza yaya kussu*

17 *Jōtai sono mama*
Migi mae keage

Upper body as is/Right front snap kick

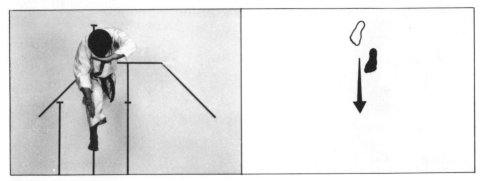

17. *Hidari ashi-dachi*

18 Migi ken migi sokumen jōdan uchi uke
Hidari ken hidari sokumen gedan uke

Upper level block, inside outward, to right side with right fist/
Downward block to left side with left fist

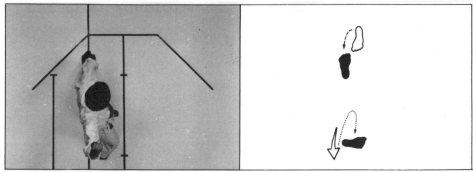

18. Migi kōkutsu-dachi

Migi shutō gedan uchi-komi
Hidari shō migi kata ue nagashi-uke

Lower level strike with right sword hand/Sweeping block, left palm to right shoulder Left palm diagonally upward.

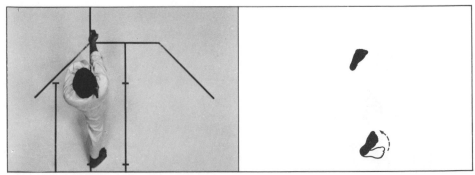

19. Hidari hiza kussu

20 *Hidari ken gedan ni nobasu*
Migi ken migi koshi

Left fist extended downward/Right fist at right side Execute
slowly, as if wringing something out.

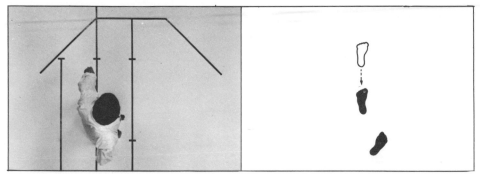

20. *Hidari mae shizen-tai*

21 *Migi shutō jōdan yoko mawashi-uchi*
Hidari shō hitai mae jōdan uke

Upper level horizontal strike with right sword hand/Upper level block, left palm in front of forehead/Reverse half-front-facing position

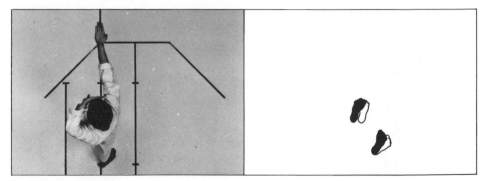

21. Hidari hiza kussu

22 | *Jōtai sono mama Migi mae keage*

Upper body as is/Right front snap kick

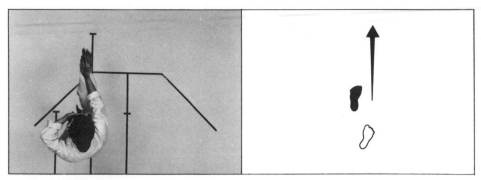

22. *Hidari ashi-dachi*

23 Migi ken migi sokumen jōdan uchi uke
Hidari ken hidari sokumen gedan uke

Upper level block, inside outward, to right side with right fist/
Downward block to left side with left fist

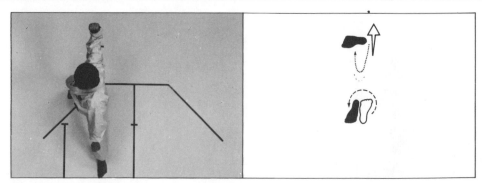

23. Migi kōkutsu-dachi

24 Migi shutō gedan uchi-komi
Hidari shō migi kata ue nagashi-uke

Lower level strike with right sword hand/Sweeping block, left palm to right shoulder Feet in same position.

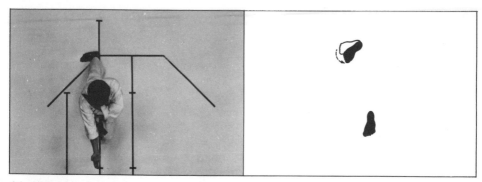

24. Hidari hiza kussu

25 | *Hidari ken gedan ni nobasu Migi ken migi koshi*

26 | *Ryō ken migi koshi kamae/Hidari ken migi ken ue*

Left fist extended downward/Right fist at right side

Both fists right side kamae

 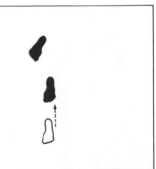

25. *Hidari mae shizen-tai*

27

*Hidari uraken jōdan yoko mawashi-uchi
Hidari yoko keage*

*Upper level horizontal strike with left back-fist/Left side snap
kick*

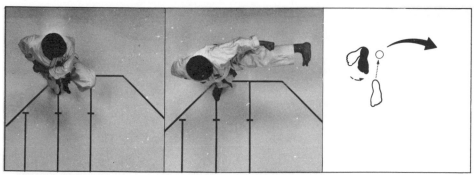

26. *Migi ashi-dachi*   27.

Migi empi mae uchi

Right elbow strike to the front   Strike left palm.

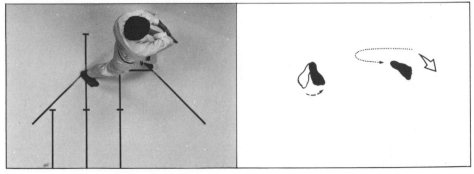

28. Hidari zenkutsu-dachi

29 *Ryō ken hidari koshi*

Both fists at left side   Rotate hips to the right, face right side.

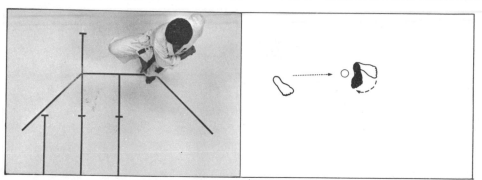

29. *Hidari ashi-dachi*

30 Migi uraken jōdan yoko mawashi-uchi/ Migi yoko keage

Upper level horizontal strike with right back-fist/Right side snap kick

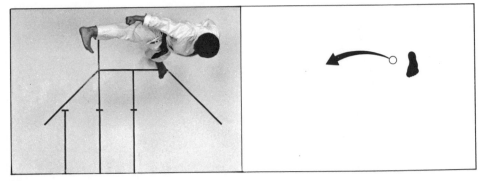

30.

31 — Hidari empi mae uchi

Left elbow strike to the front

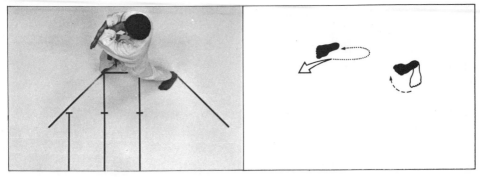

31. *Migi zenkutsu-dachi*

32 *Hidari shutō uke*

Left sword hand block With feet in place, turn hips left, face to the rear.

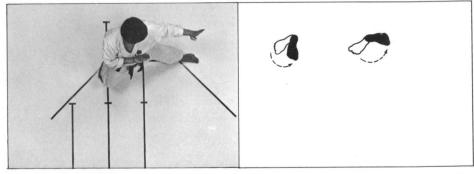

32. Migi kōkutsu-dachi

33 *Migi shutō uke*

Right sword hand block With left leg as pivot, advance right leg one step diagonally forward.

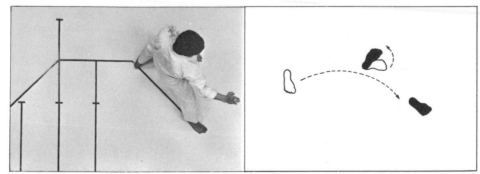

33. *Hidari kōkutsu-dachi*

34 *Migi shutō uke*

Right sword hand block With left leg as pivot, rotate hips to the right.

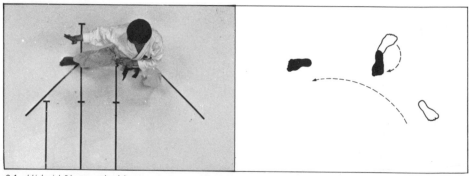

34. Hidari kōkutsu-dachi

Left sword hand block With right leg as pivot, move left leg diagonally forward.

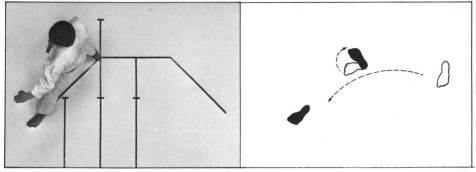

35. Migi kōkutsu-dachi

36 Migi shutō jōdan yoko mawashi uchi
Hidari shō hitai mae jōdan uke

Upper level horizontal strike with right sword hand/Upper level block, left palm in front of forehead/Reverse half-front-facing position

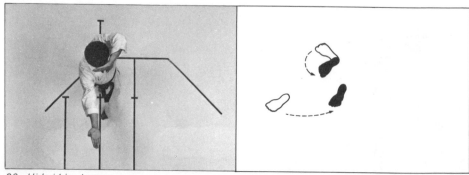

36. Hidari hiza kussu

37 *Migi mae keage*

Right front snap kick

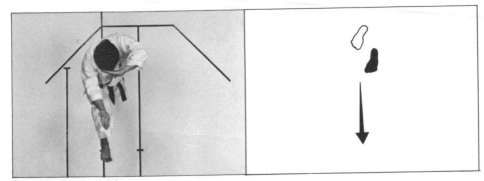

37. *Hidari ashi-dachi*

38 Migi uraken tate mawashi-uchi
Hidari ken hidari koshi

Right back-fist vertical strike/Left fist at left side   Rotate both
fists vertically.

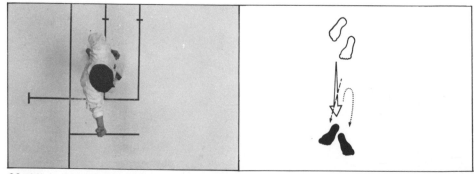

38. *Migi ashi mae kōsa-dachi*

39 *Migi chūdan uchi uke*

Right middle level block, inside outward Keeping the elbow in place, return the right fist from under the left elbow.

39. Migi zenkutsu-dachi

Left middle level straight punch

 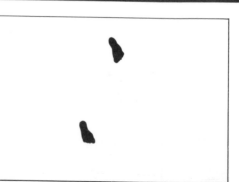

40.

41 *Migi chūdan choku-zuki*

Right middle level straight punch

41.

42 Migi ura-zuki/Hidari shō migi tekubi yoko-zoe Migi hiza ate

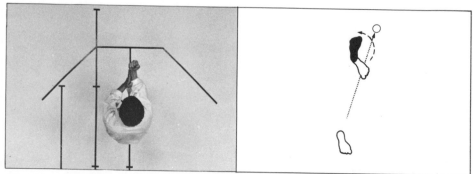

Right close punch/Left palm at right wrist/Right knee strike
Rotate hips to the left, turn to the rear.

42. Hidari ashi-dachi

Ryō shō hiji tate-fuse

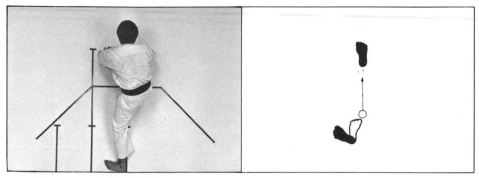

Both hands, elbows take cover Right foot forward, go to ground, hands turning inward. Look about four meters ahead.

43. *Migi ashi mae fuse*

Hidari shutō gedan barai
Migi shutō mune mae kamae

Left sword hand downward block/Right sword hand in front of chest kamae Right palm upward, left palm downward.

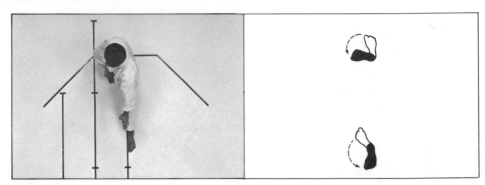

44. Migi kōkutsu-dachi (hikume)

Right sword hand block   Advance right leg one step forward.

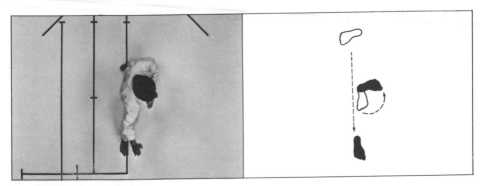

45. Hidari kōkutsu-dachi

Hidari chūdan uchi uke

Left middle level block, inside outward   With left leg as pivot,
rotate hips to the left.

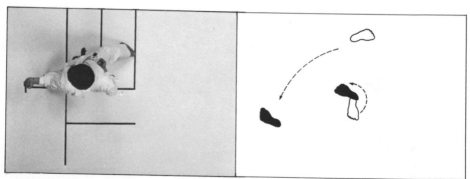

46. *Hidari zenkutsu-dachi*

47 Migi chūdan choku-zuki

Right middle level straight punch

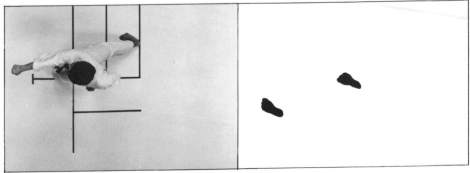

47.

48 *Migi chūdan uchi uke*

Right middle level block, inside outward Turn hips to the right.

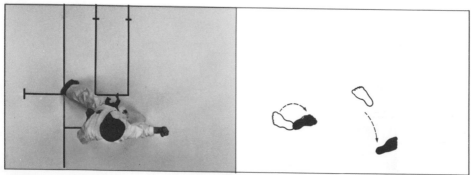

48. *Migi zenkutsu-dachi*

49 Hidari chūdan choku-zuki

50 Migi chūdan choku-zuki

Left middle level straight punch

Right middle level straight punch

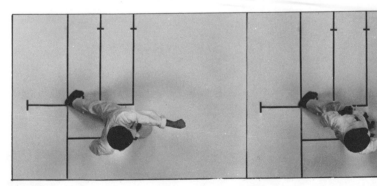

49.

50.

Both fists at left side With upper body as is, raise right foot to the side of the left knee.

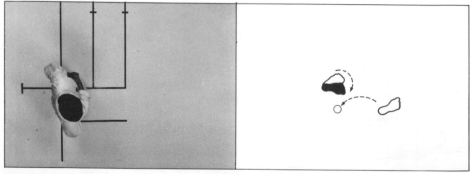

51. *Hidari ashi-dachi*

52 *Migi uraken jōdan yoko mawashi-uchi*
Migi yoko keage

Upper level horizontal strike with right back-fist / Right side snap kick

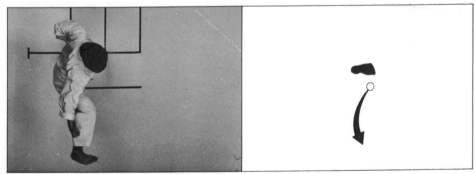

52.

Hidari shutō uke

Left sword hand block Turn hips to the left, face to the rear.
Bring kicking foot down to the rear.

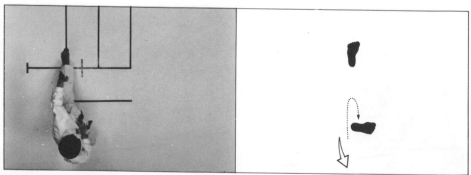

53. Migi kōkutsu-dachi

54 *Migi nukite chūdan-zuki*
Hidari shō osae-uke

Right spear hand middle level punch/Pressing block with left palm Left palm under right elbow. Advance right foot forward.

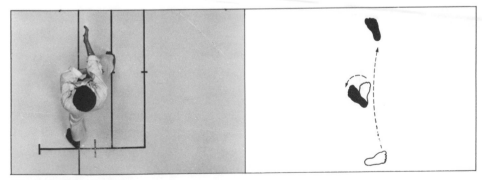

54. Migi zenkutsu-dachi

55 Hidari uraken tate mawashi-uchi
Migi ken migi koshi

Vertical strike with left back-fist/Right fist at right side   With right foot as pivot, turn left, align feet. Twist right wrist to the right and use this motion as "center" in turning the upper body.

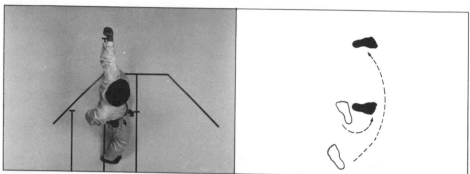

55. Kiba-dachi

56 Hidari kentsui chūdan yoko uchi
Sono mama hidari ni yori-ashi

Middle level horizontal strike with left hammer fist/Yori-ashi to the left   Swing left fist from in front of right shoulder.

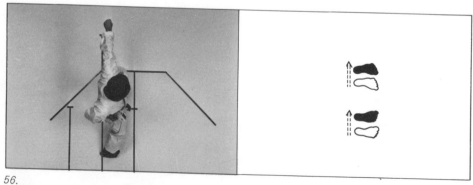

57 *Migi empi mae uchi*

Right elbow strike to the front   Strike left palm.

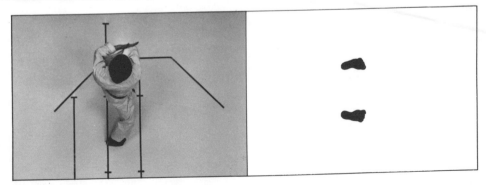

57.

58 *Ryō ken hidari koshi*

Both fists at left side   Right fist (back frontward) on top.

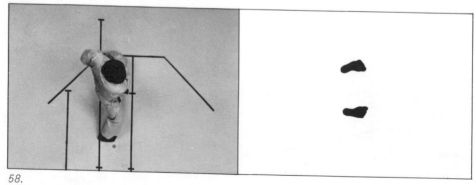

58.

59 *Migi gedan barai*

Right downward block

59.

Downward block with left fist/Upward swing with right fist
With right leg as pivot, turn hips widely to the right. Raise left

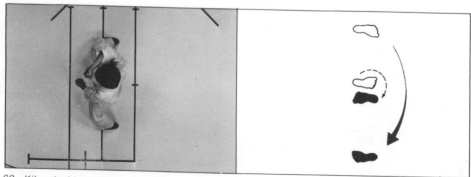

60. Kiba-dachi

knee high for strong stamping kick. Execute hand movements at
the same time as hip rotation.

61 Migi ken otoshi-zuki

Downward punch with right fist behind left fist, crossing wrists.　Bring right fist (back outward)

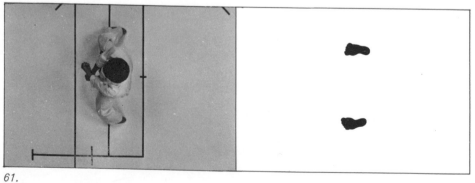

61.

62 *Ryō shō atama ue kōsa uke*

Cross block, both hands above head Backs of hands facing each other. Straighten knees to come to *shizen-tai*.

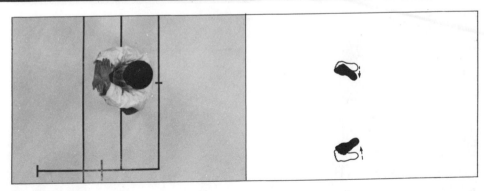

62. Shizen-tai

Ryō ken ago mae kōsa

Both fists crossing in front of jaw   With the right leg as pivot, rotate hips widely to the right. Clench both fists and lower them slowly.

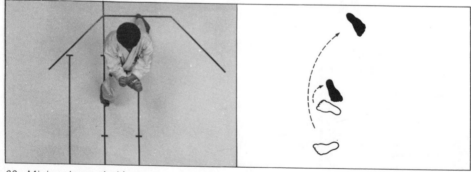

63. Migi zenkutsu-dachi

Two level kick

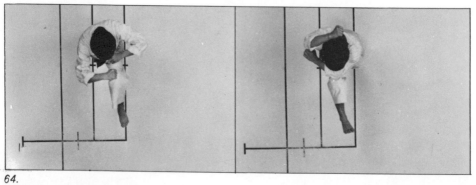

64.

65 Migi uraken tate mawashi-uchi   Yame
Hidari ken hidari koshi

Vertical strike with right back-fist/Left fist
at left side

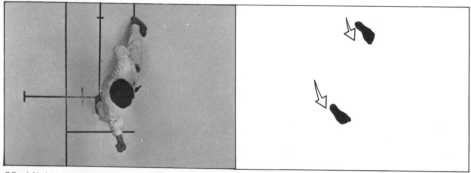

65. Migi zenkutsu-dachi

In a movement complementary to the wide opening of the arms
at the beginning, make a wide, circular closing movement.

KANKŪ: IMPORTANT POINTS

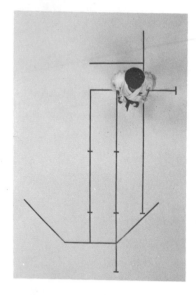

Kankū is one of the longest kata in karate, and its present name comes from the first and second movements, "looking at the sky." Its earlier name, Kūshankū, goes back to Kung Siang Chün, who was a member of a diplomatic mission during the Ming dynasty and an expert in Chinese boxing.

From it one should learn to dispose of a variety of attacks made by a number of opponents, coming from four or even eight directions, for it abounds in variations. It is the kata the Gichin Funakoshi most liked to see performed.

In it, of course, are techniques of fast and slow tempo, the dynamics of strength and the expansion and contraction of the body. From it must also be mastered changes of direction, jumping and going to ground.

The *embusen* is in the shape of an I, with the vertical line extending above the upper horizontal line.

Sixty-five movements. About ninety seconds.

1. Movements 1 and 2: These are for regulating breathing. They also have the purpose of showing that one is not armed and of protecting the groin. The feeling is of describing a large circle representing the sky.
2. Movements 10 and 11: Without moving the upper body, draw the left foot directly under it. Counterattack with a side kick and back-fist strike at the time of changing direction. This is the same as Movement 7 of Heian 2.
3. Movements 17, 18, 19: Execute continuously and rapidly. Effectively use snap to bring back the kicking leg. Rotate hips strongly and fast.
4. Movement 38: After jumping forward, support the body weight on the bent right leg, lightly bring the left foot in back of the right for the crossed-feet stance. At the same time, extend the left hand, as if to grab something, and pull it back to the hip. Strike to the upper level with the right back-fist, as if sliding it from the abdomen to the chest. Hand and foot movements at the same time. This is the same point as in Movement 13 of Heian 4.

5

6

5. Movement 42: With left leg as pivot, reverse direction and at the same time raise right knee high. Raise the fists on either side of the right thigh. Align the left fist by the right wrist and strike with both fists (back of right fist downward). The right elbow should be about a fist-width above the right knee.

6. Movement 43: This is the posture of taking cover. Bending the right leg, place both hands lightly on the floor. Lift the head, as if to stare at something about four meters ahead. Be careful not to raise the hips high. Continue rapidly from Movement 42 to 43.

8

7. Movement 51: Since the hips were turned in Movement 50, they are already in position for the side kick. Without moving the left foot, raise the right foot next to the left knee to be in position for the side kick and back-fist strike.

8. Movement 55: With the right arm twisted to the right over the right shoulder, use the elbow as the center of the movement and turn the upper body left and to the front. The right leg is the pivot leg. Move the left leg to the front. This is useful when your right arm has been grasped by the opponent. Instead of trying to free it, move your body around your right arm.

10

9. Movement 60: The rising strike of the right fist has no special meaning. It is a counterbalance to the wide forceful downward strike of the left fist.

10. Movements 62 and 63: After the upper level cross block, turn body to the right with fists as the center of the movement. Grabbing the opponent's wrists, lower both hands.

11. Movement 65: After the two level kick, since there is the feeling of grasping something in front with the left hand, withdraw it to the left hip. Strike to the upper level with the right vertical back-fist in a movement sliding from the abdomen up past the chest. Execute the hand movements at the same time the feet land.

12. *Yame*: With right leg as pivot, turn to the right. While turning the left hand, as if for a sweeping block, align the left foot with the right. Lower both hands naturally.

GLOSSARY

Roman numerals refer to other volumes in this series: I, Comprehensive; II, Fundamentals; III, Kumite 1; IV, Kumite 2; V, Heian, Tekki.

ago: jaw
ashi: foot, leg
atama: head

chūdan: middle level
chūdan choku-zuki: middle level straight punch, 27, 75; I, 66
chūdan soto uke: middle level block, outside inward, 20; II, 20; IV, 126
chūdan uchi uke: middle level block, inside outward, 17, 74; I, 59; II, 22; V, 40
chūdan uke: middle level block, 31, 81; I, 59, 96; II, 90, 106; V, 28
chūdan yoko uchi: middle level side strike, 124
chūdan-zuki: middle level punch, 41, 84; V, 32

dan: 13

embusen: performance line, 13, 64, 138; I, 94
empi: elbow
empi chūdan mae uchi: middle level elbow strike to the front, 47
empi mae uchi: front elbow strike, 96; V, 85

fumidachi: 65; II, 68; V, 58
fumikomi: stamping kick, 128; I, 87; II, 60, 68; III, 33; V, 60
furiage: upward swing, 128, 141

gedan: lower level
gedan barai: downward block, 48, 112; I, 56; II, 106; V, 17
gedan uchi-komi: lower level strike, 42, 88, 138
gedan uchi uke: lower level block, inside outward, 56, 65, 93
gedan uke: downward block, 43, 65, 87, 138, 140; V, 50

gyaku hanmi: reverse half-front-facing position, 24, 85, 138; II, 24; V, 40

hachinoji-dachi: open-leg stance, 25, 68; I, 29; V, 16
haiwan: upper side of forearm, backarm
hasami uchi: scissors strike, 40, 65
heisoku-dachi: informal attention stance, 16; I, 29; V, 50
hidari: left
hidari ashi-dachi: left leg stance, 36, 79; V, 35
hidari hiza kussu: left knee bent, 30, 76
hidari mae hiza kussu: left front knee bent, 42
hidari mae hiza yaya kussu: left front knee slightly bent, 35, 85
hidari mae shizen-tai: left front natural position, 89
hiji: elbow
hitai: forehead
hiza: knee
hiza ate: knee strike, 110

ikken hisatsu: to kill with one blow, 11

jōdan: upper level
jōdan uchi uke: upper level block, inside outward, 43, 87
jōdan uke: upper level block, 72; I, 57; II, 106; V, 46
jōdan-zuki: upper level punch, 51
jōtai: upper body

kafukubu: abdomen
kake-uke: hooking block, 45; I, 64; V, 83
kamae: posture, 12, 25, 65, 72; III, 14; IV, 40; V, 32
kasaneru: put one on top of another
kata: shoulder
kekomi: thrust kick, 36; I, 86; II, 82,

135; III, 50

ken: fist

kentsui: hammer fist

kiai: 14

kiba-dachi: straddle-leg stance, 44, 122; I, 32; II, 52; V, 54

kime: 11; I, 50; III, 15; IV, 118; V, 61

kōkutsu-dachi: back stance, 31, 72; I, 31; II, 52; III, 40; V, 26

kōkutsu-dachi (hikume): back stance (low), 112

kōsa: cross

kōsa-dachi: crossed-feet stance, 138; II, 52; V, 68

kōsa-uke: cross block, 131, 141

koshi: hips, side, I, 52; II, 13

kumite: sparring, 10, 13; I, 111

kyū: 13

mae: front, to the front, in front of

mae keage: front snap kick, 86, 138; I, 86; II, 88; III, 67; V, 41

migi: right

migi ashi-dachi: right leg stance, 17, 94; V, 66

migi ashi mae fuse: right leg in front, take cover, 111

migi hiza kussu: right knee bent, 30, 78

mikazuki-geri: crescent kick, 46, 65; IV, 52, 64; V, 84

morote jōdan uke: upper level block with both hands, 39

mune: chest

musubi-dachi: informal attention stance, 12; I, 29

nagashi-uke: sweeping block, 42, 88, 138; I, 62; IV, 82; V, 33

naname: diagonally

nidan geri: two-level kick, 134; I, 90

nobasu: extend

nukite: spear hand

osae-uke: pressing block, 84; V, 129

otoshi-zuki: downward punch, 130

ryō: both

sayū: left and right

shizen-tai: natural position, 16, 68, 131; I, 28; V, 16

shō: palm

shutō: sword hand

shutō uke: sword hand block, 31, 66, 82; I, 60; II, 118; IV, 138; V, 26

sokumen: side

sokutō: sword foot

sun-dome: arresting a technique, 11

tanden: center of gravity, 12

tate-fuse: taking cover, going to ground, 111, 139

tate mawashi-uchi: vertical strike, 106, 138, 139, 141; I, 75; II, 129; V, 18

tate shutō uke: vertical sword hand block, 26, 74; I, 61

tekubi: wrist

tsukami uke: grasping block, 35, 64; V, 115

tsukamiyose: grasping-pulling, 36, 64

uchi uke: block, inside ouwtard, 18, 74, 138; I, 59; II, 22; V, 40

ude: arm

ue: above, over

uraken: back-fist

ura-zuki: close punch, 51, 110, 139; I, 70; IV, 44; V, 98

yama-zuki: wide U punch, 51, 65; I, 72

yame: stop

yōi: readiness, 16, 68

yoko keage: side snap kick, 80, 138, 139; I, 87; II, 135; V, 35

yoko mawashi-uchi: horizontal strike, 80, 138, 139; I, 75; II, 129; V, 35

yori-ashi: sliding the feet, 41, 124; II, 70; III, 100; V, 60

zanshin: state of relaxed alertness, 13; III, 26

zenkutsu-dachi: front stance, 18, 89; I, 30; II, 18, 52; V, 17